Nights of Nature

Ian Rohr

Brainwaves Purple
Nightmares of Nature
ISBN 978 1 86509 832 6 (Paperback)
ISBN 978 1 86509 851 7 (Hardback)

All rights reserved. No part of this publication may be reproduced, stored in a retrieval system or transmitted in any form or by any means, electronic, mechanical, photocopying, recording, or otherwise, without the prior written permission of the publisher.

Copyright © 2003 Blake Publishing
Reprinted 2008

Published by Blake Education Pty Ltd
ABN 074 266 023
Locked Bag 2022
Glebe NSW 2037
Ph: (02) 8585 4085
Fax: (02) 8585 4058
Email: mail@blake.com.au
Website: www.blake.com.au

Series publisher: Sharon Dalgleish
Designer: Cliff Watt
Illustrators: Rob Mancini, Lloyd Foye, and Cliff Watt
Photo research: Tracey Gibson

Picture credits: Picture Credits; pg 6-9 photolibrary.com; pg 11 (top) Kathie Atkinson/Auscape, (bottom right and left) APL/Corbis; pg 14 (bottom) photolibrary.com; pg 15 (bottom) photolibrary.com; pg 18 (bottom) APL/Corbis; pg 19 (top) François Gohier/Auscape; pg 23 (bottom) APL/Corbis.

Printed by SNP Security Printing

Contents

- **Tiny Attackers** 4
  - Bloodsuckers! 6
  - Itsy Bitsy—but Mighty Nasty 8

- **SSSSnakes** 12
  - Taking a Bite 14
  - Not So Tight! 18

- **First One In the Water . . . Is Dinner!** . . 20
  - Hidden Dangers 22
  - Open Wide 26

      Fact File 30
      Glossary 31
      Index 32

Tiny Attackers

Imagine a tiny creature that can crawl up your nose to suck your blood.

It then grows so bloated on your blood that it blocks off the air inside your nose, so you suffocate and die. Such a creature does exist. It's a leech. But grazing animals, such as cattle, are the ones at risk—not us. Even so, leeches still make most of us squirm.

What gives you nightmares? Giant spiders? Snakes that kill with one bite? There are lots of little horrors around us—things that bite, or sting. Some are just a nuisance, but others can kill. So open your eyes, watch your step, and have a close look at some of nature's mini-monsters.

BLOODSUCKERS

There are creatures out there that want your blood, and they are well designed to just come and get it.

Hanging on Like a Leech

Leeches live everywhere, from deserts to polar regions. And some do like to suck on human blood. The bite is painless, so you probably won't even know it's latched on to you. A leech busily sucks out ten times its own weight in blood, growing up to five times bigger until it's full. Full of your blood, it drops off and can now live for a year before it must feed again.

The largest leech is the giant Amazon leech. This is just a baby—they can grow to 46 cm!

This magnified mouth of a leech has three rows of teeth to cut a Y shape in its victim. The skin at the wound then peels back to let the blood flow out.

Hordes on Your Head

Feeling itchy? A little bit scratchy? If so, you might be one of the millions of people who've become a home for the head louse. Like leeches, lice are **parasites**. The head louse lives on our heads, and off our blood. Sometimes the only way to get rid of them is to shave your head!

Still can't get rid of these humans!

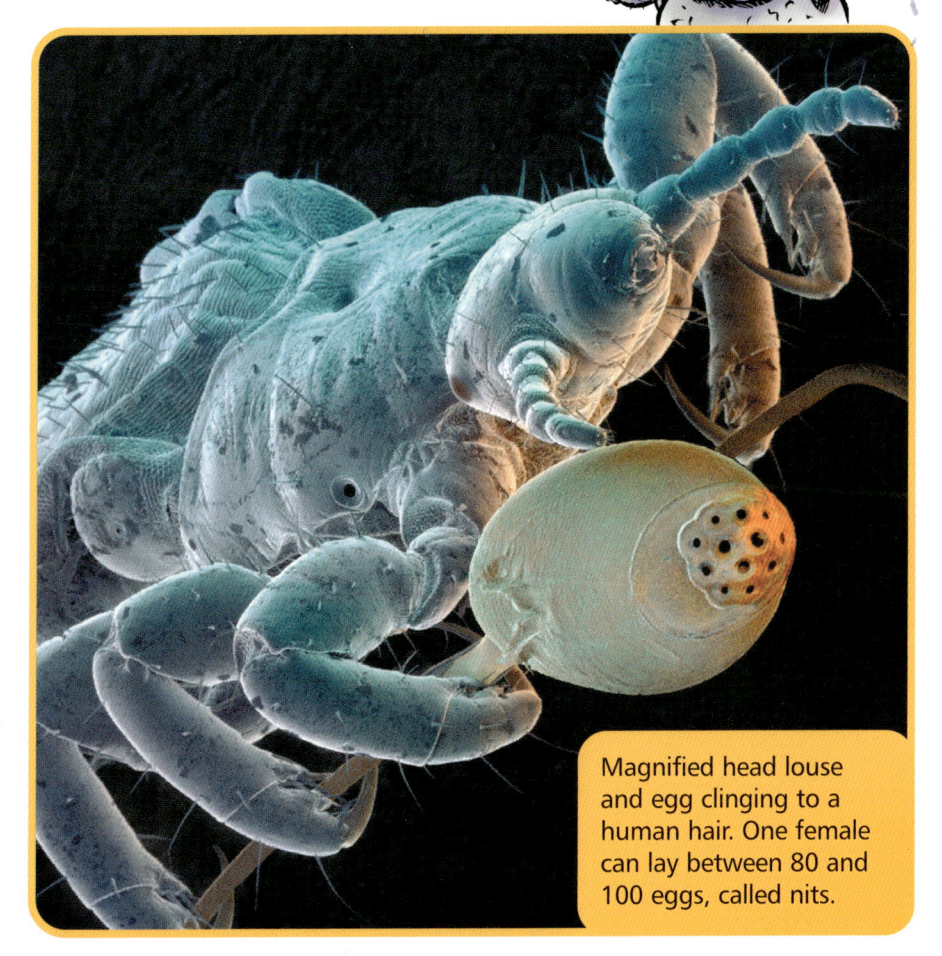

Magnified head louse and egg clinging to a human hair. One female can lay between 80 and 100 eggs, called nits.

Itsy Bitsy—but Mighty Nasty

Do sticky webs and eight hairy legs make you scream? You're not alone. Fear of spiders is common. Most people don't need to have had a bad experience to still be very afraid of them.

What's Big and Hairy?

The venom of the Goliath bird-eating spider is not very poisonous, and a bite is said to hurt no more than a needle does. But this spider, found in the rainforests of South America, makes up for it in size, bluff and a don't-mess-with-me appearance. The hairy Goliath bird-eating spider is big enough to wrap itself, and its two-and-a-half centimetre-long fangs, around your face. At 25 centimetres across, if one were sitting on your dinner plate there'd be no room for any vegetables.

Not spiders again!

Nasty Surprises

If walking into a web has you clawing at your face frantic to avoid a spider, be careful if you're ever in a tropical forest. Orb-web spiders weave webs that can stretch 10 metres from the treetops to the ground, and measure 7 metres around. And the silk spun by the female golden orb-web spider is, weight for weight, five times stronger than steel. The webs are strong enough to catch and hold a bird, and locals use them to make fishing nets and traps.

A female golden orb-web spider producing silk. Scientists are studying the silk to try to make fibres that are as strong.

This black and yellow spider is a type of orb-web spider. It's caught a hummingbird for dinner.

Silk

Spinneret

Deadlier than Most

Most spiders curl up and play dead or scuttle away if disturbed. But the Brazilian wandering spider will stand and fight. People pushing them away with sticks or brooms are horrified when the spiders run up the handle to bite them. These spiders share urban areas with people, and are responsible for thousands of bites each year.

With fangs that can pierce fingernails and attitude to spare, male funnel-web spiders aren't big, but they're bad. These aggressive spiders are found in eastern Australia, and they're fighters who aren't at all afraid of attacking a human. Their **venom** produces immediate, severe pain, followed by extreme sweating, muscle spasms and cramps throughout the body. If the bite is bad enough, you could end up in a coma or die. Since 1927 there have been 14 reported deaths from encounters with Sydney funnel-webs alone.

TOP 5 DEADLIEST SPIDERS

Sydney funnel-web spider

Australia

Brazilian wandering spider

Central and South America

wolf spider

Central and South America

black widow spider

worldwide

recluse spider

worldwide

The funnel-web spider raises its head to attack, then stabs by moving its head down.

This funnel-web spider is being milked for its venom. This will be used to produce antivenom to give to people bitten by the spiders.

Wandering spiders do not build a web. They actively hunt their prey on the forest floor.

11

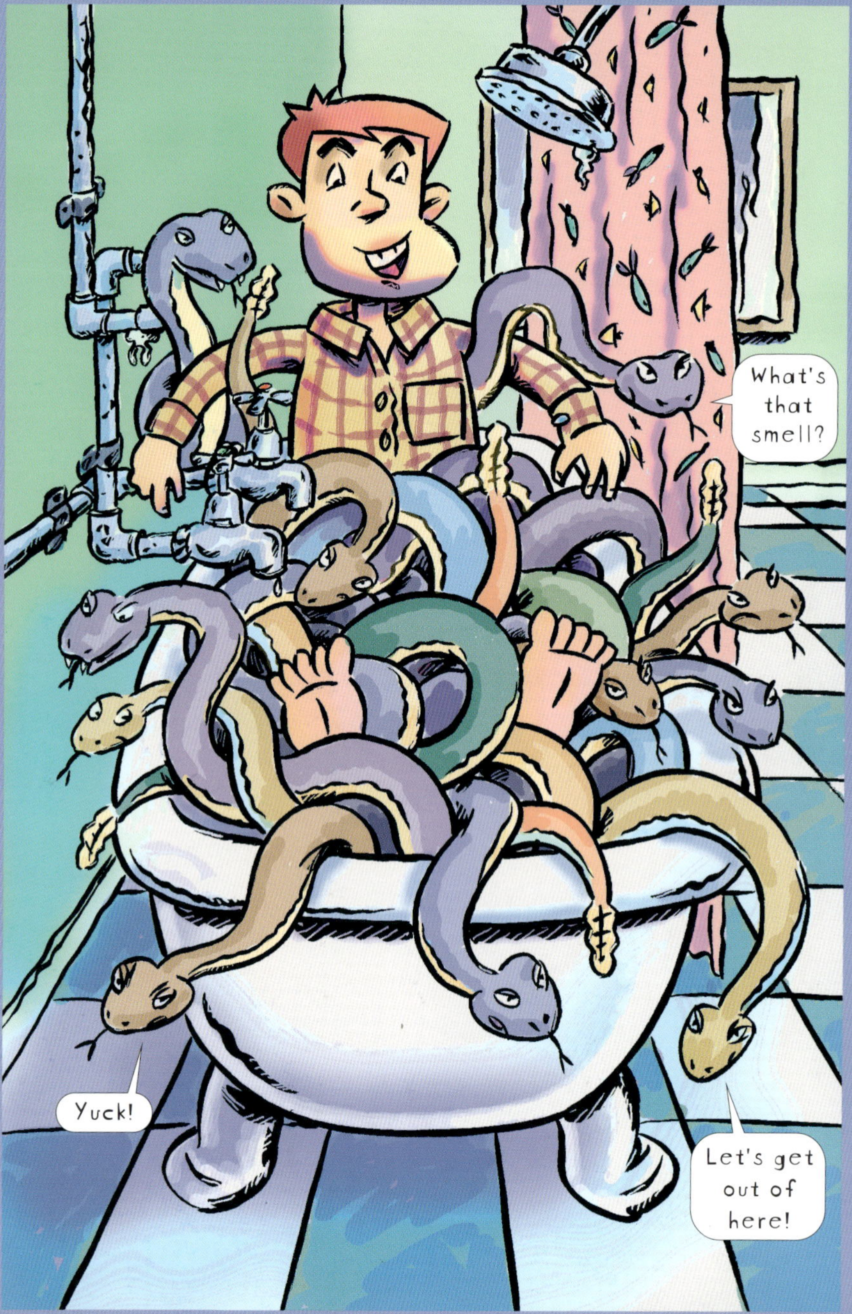
What's that smell?
Yuck!
Let's get out of here!

Sssssnakes

Would you take a bath in a tub full of rattlesnakes? The world record is ten seconds!

In 1999, two American snake handlers filled two tubs with 75 western diamondback rattlesnakes each . . . and then climbed in themselves. Then they stayed there for ten seconds to set a new world record. They must have known what they were doing, because they didn't get bitten.

For most people this would be their worst nightmare. For hundreds of years humans have feared, hated, and killed these creatures. Snakes live on every continent in the world except Antarctica. But most people would not even consider going near these slithering strips of danger.

Australia's taipan has the most toxic venom and is considered the world's deadliest snake.

TAKING A BITE

Our horror of snakes far outweighs any real threat they pose to us. But with two sharp fangs and a mouth to swallow dinner whole, it is no wonder snakes have a bad reputation.

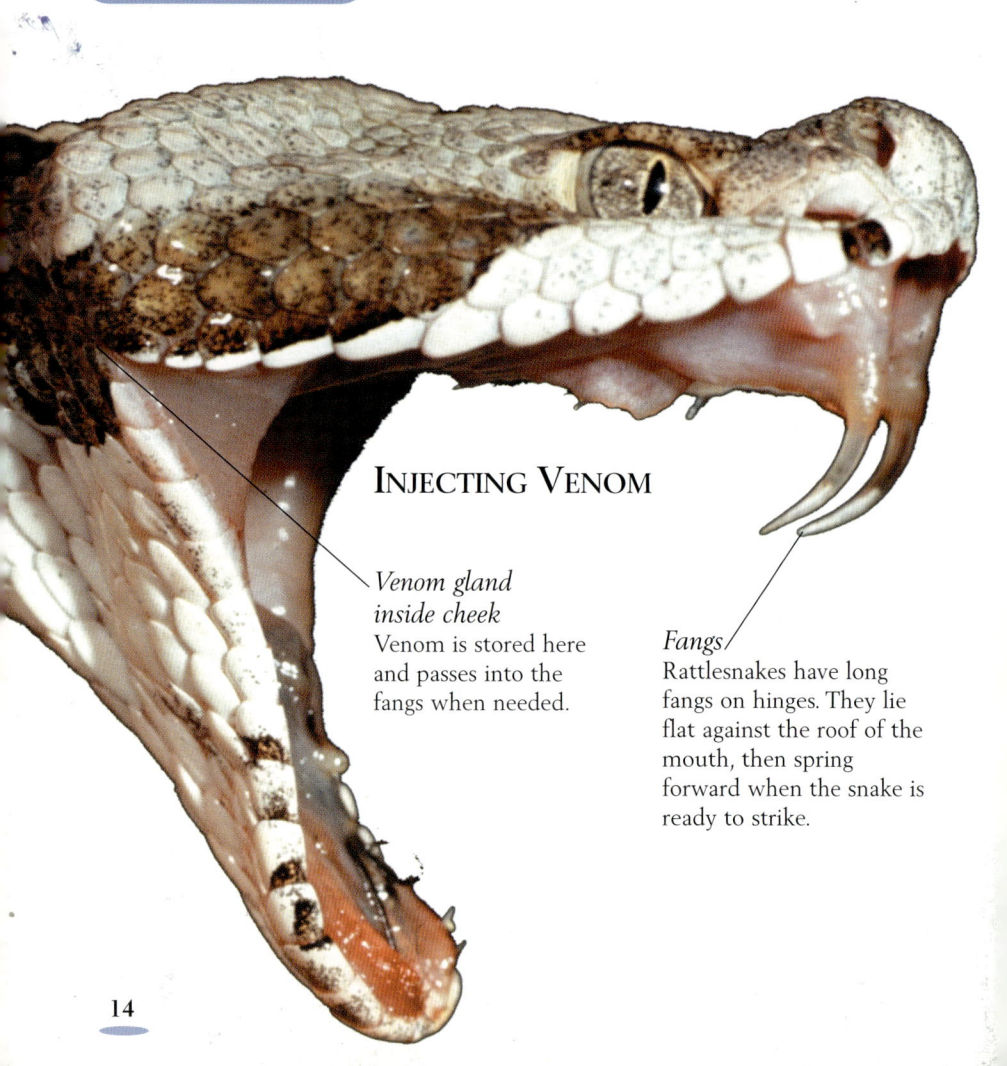

INJECTING VENOM

Venom gland inside cheek
Venom is stored here and passes into the fangs when needed.

Fangs
Rattlesnakes have long fangs on hinges. They lie flat against the roof of the mouth, then spring forward when the snake is ready to strike.

Fancy Fangs

Some of the deadliest snakes have long **fangs** at the front of their mouths. They use the fangs to inject venom into their prey. When the snake bites, the liquid is released from the venom glands, and travels down the hollow fangs into the victim. It is these snakes that are most dangerous to humans. The long fangs can pierce our skin and inject venom directly into our bloodstream. The Gaboon viper from tropical Africa has the longest fangs and can inject poison up to 50 millimetres under the skin.

The tiger snake is very aggressive and kills more people in Australia than any other.

Deadly snakes, like this taipan, are milked to help produce antivenom.

Here Comes Dinner—Gulp!

Snakes with venom use it to stop their prey from struggling so they can then gulp it down—in one piece. One type of venom works to **paralyse** the victim by attacking its **nervous system**. Another type works by destroying the victim's muscles. If the prey does manage to get away, the venom will still begin to work. The snake can follow the animal's heat trail and still get a meal.

Snakes have flexible mouths and jaws that can stretch to swallow animals much larger than themselves. Depending on the size of the snake, a snake's diet may include insects, rats, frogs, other reptiles and even pigs or goats. Some frogs try to defend themselves by inflating their mouths with air. But snakes just grab them from behind and push all the air out of the frog's mouth.

Burp!

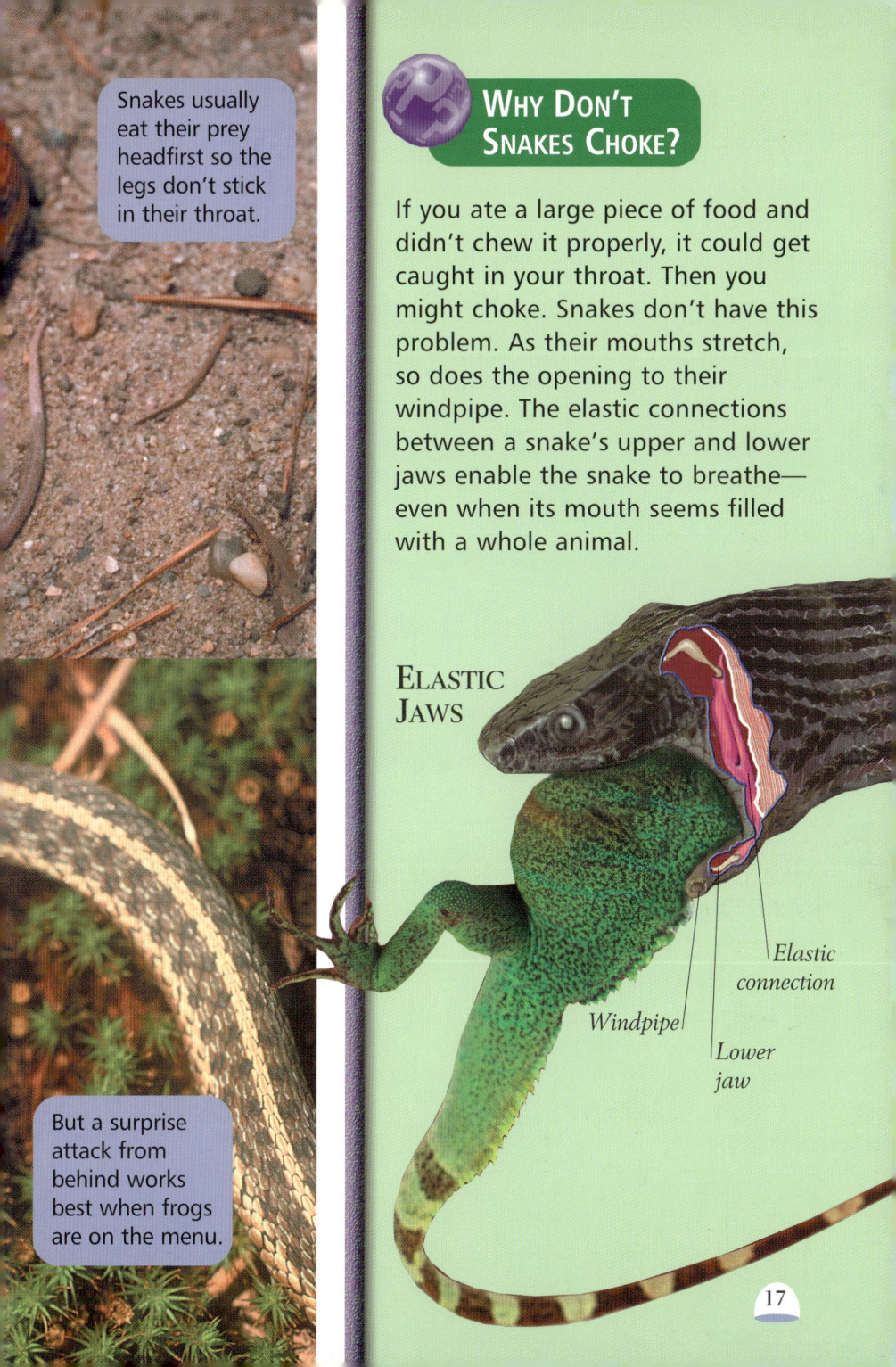

Snakes usually eat their prey headfirst so the legs don't stick in their throat.

But a surprise attack from behind works best when frogs are on the menu.

Why Don't Snakes Choke?

If you ate a large piece of food and didn't chew it properly, it could get caught in your throat. Then you might choke. Snakes don't have this problem. As their mouths stretch, so does the opening to their windpipe. The elastic connections between a snake's upper and lower jaws enable the snake to breathe—even when its mouth seems filled with a whole animal.

Elastic Jaws

Elastic connection
Windpipe
Lower jaw

Boa constrictor

Not So Tight!

Not all snakes use venom to kill their prey—some just squeeze and dinner is served.

Last Breath

A lightning-fast ambush from the bushes or the water is how the South American anaconda first grabs its prey. It latches on with sharp teeth and then wraps itself around and around. Then it lets the prey do most of the work. Each time the trapped animal breathes out, the anaconda tightens its grip. Soon, usually within minutes, the snake is wrapped around so tightly that breathing becomes impossible for the victim. It **suffocates** and dies.

A boa constrictor squeezes its body around a rat to kill it.

This 4.5 m anaconda has a stomach bulging with dinner.

Ooops! I've got a grip on myself.

Big Feed
When the anaconda is sure that the prey is dead, it uncoils itself, locates the head with its flickering tongue, and begins the long, slow business of swallowing and digesting. The prey is squeezed into the snake's stomach by strong muscles. It may take days for the snake to digest a pig or antelope, but it won't need to eat again for up to a month.

THE SIZE OF THE BEAST
Pythons and boa constrictors also squeeze their prey to death.

human
carpet python — 2 m
boa constrictor — 4.5 m
anaconda — 10 m

0 m   2 m   4 m   6 m   8 m   10 m

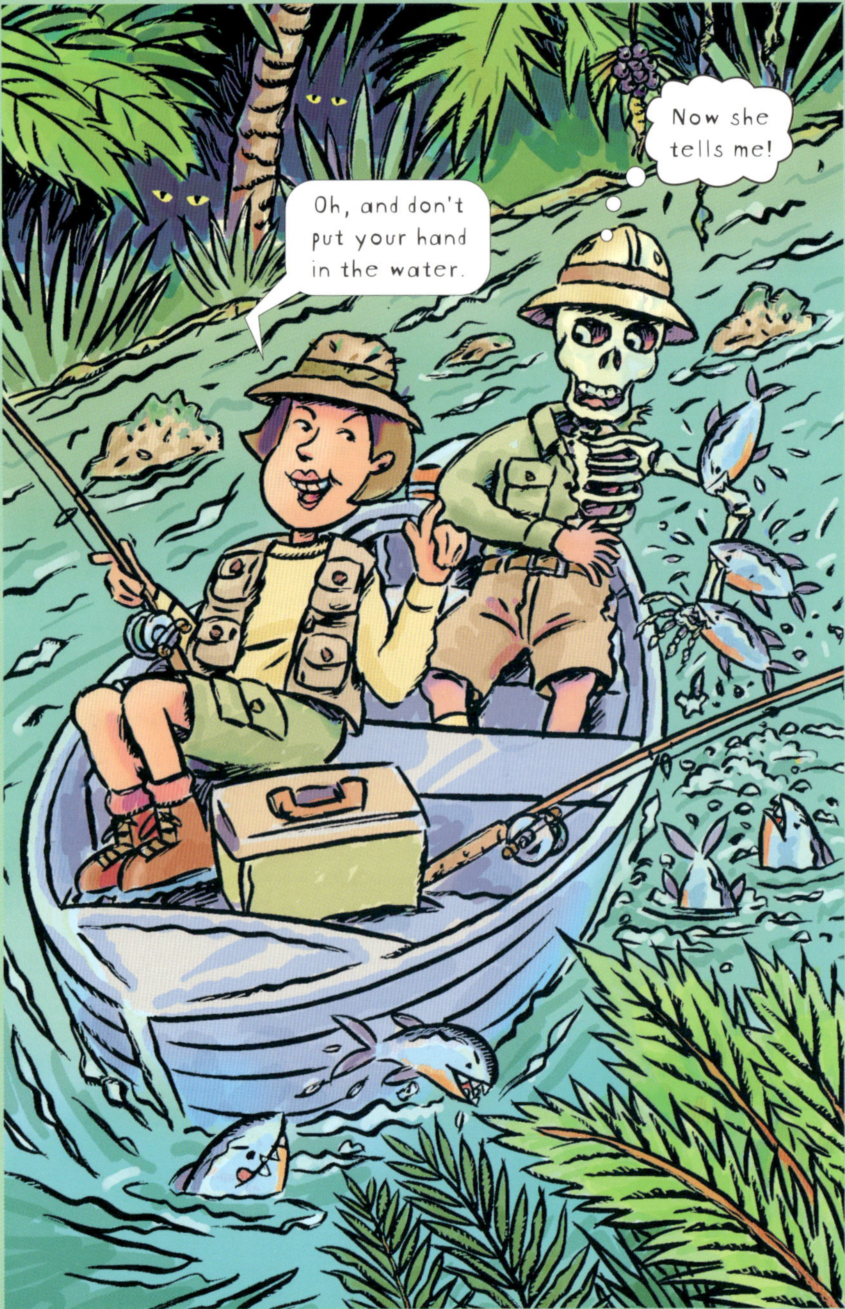
Oh, and don't put your hand in the water.
Now she tells me!

First One in the Water... Is Dinner!

If you want to make it into the record books, get eaten by piranhas.

These little fish have sharp teeth and bad reputations. There is no proof that they strip humans to the bone in seconds. But if it's ever happened, then the red-bellied piranhas did it. When the Amazon lagoons shrink in the dry season, these piranhas break their usual diet of smaller fish to eat anything that falls in the water.

Even though the piranha's not quite the bad guy people think it is, there are plenty of other nightmares waiting just below the surface. Come on in, the water's fine . . .

Hidden Dangers

When splashing about in the ocean, it pays to keep an eye out for creatures hidden in the rocks—and creatures that look like rocks!

An Eel Meal

Half-in and half-out of its hole, a moray eel hovers in the water. With teeth exposed, it waits for something edible to swim within reach. When it does, the eel shoots forward, grabs it, and wraps itself around it. It contracts its muscles from tail to head in a sudden **spasm**. Then the eel's head whips around, tearing off a big hunk of flesh. A moray eel can be as shy as it can be savage, and will retreat into its hole when something that scares it comes along.

The ever-open mouth of the moray eel makes it look fierce. But the eel does that so water will pass over its gills so it can breathe.

In areas where people and eels regularly cross paths, divers have trained eels to eat from their hands and be stroked like big underwater pets. The trouble is, the eels get used to the free lunches. Then, when the hands are empty, the eels try to eat the hands instead.

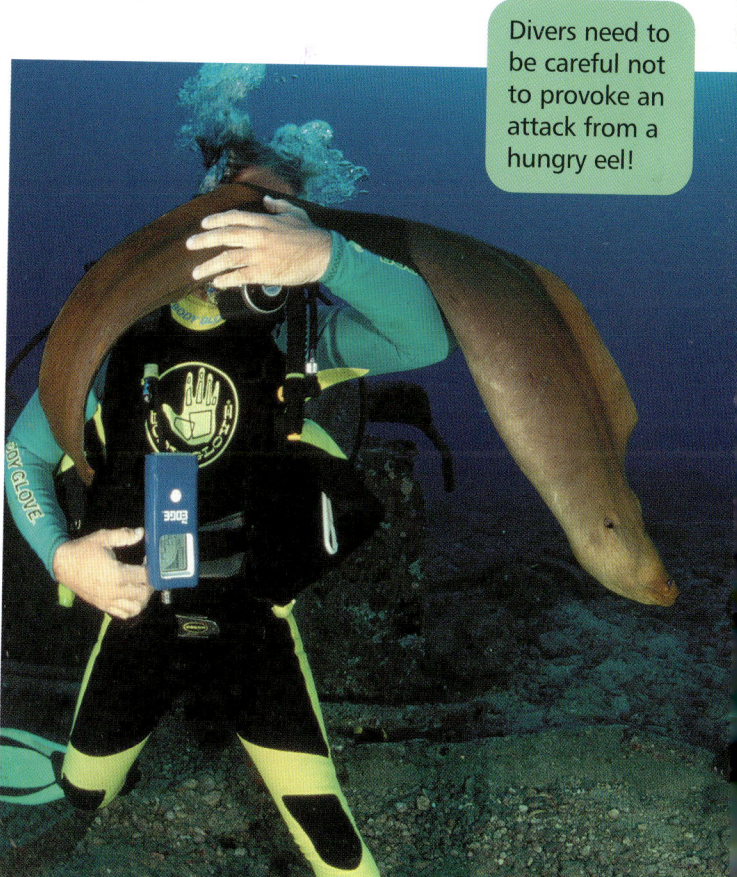

Divers need to be careful not to provoke an attack from a hungry eel!

OPEN WIDE

If you see these jaws headed your way, you had better hope it's a nightmare and not real!

Oceanic white tip shark

Bull shark

Surrounded by Sharks

Every year, humans kill about 100 million sharks. On the other hand, sharks attack about 50 to 75 people each year, and only 5 to 10 of these attacks results in death. But for those people who are fatally attacked by sharks, it is a terrifying way to die.

Great white shark

CONFIRMED SHARK ATTACKS 1580 – 2001

The earliest shark attack recorded in the International Shark Attack File happened in 1580.

Tiger shark

Of the 400 or so known **species** of shark, only 30 have been known to attack humans. And only the great white, bull, tiger and oceanic white tip sharks are regularly responsible for attacks on humans.

Asia 120 57

Australia 323 149

58

New Zealand

For 900 sailors who survived the sinking of the *USS Indianapolis* in 1945, this terror became real in the deep waters of the Pacific Ocean. The ship had sunk just after midnight and at sunrise the attacks began. The men clung together in groups in their life vests, hitting at the water and kicking their feet to try to **repel** the sharks. By the time help arrived, nearly 5 days later, only 317 had survived. Even as the men were being pulled from the sea, sharks continued to circle and strike.

Sharks can detect tiny amounts of blood in the water, and movement in the murkiest of water.

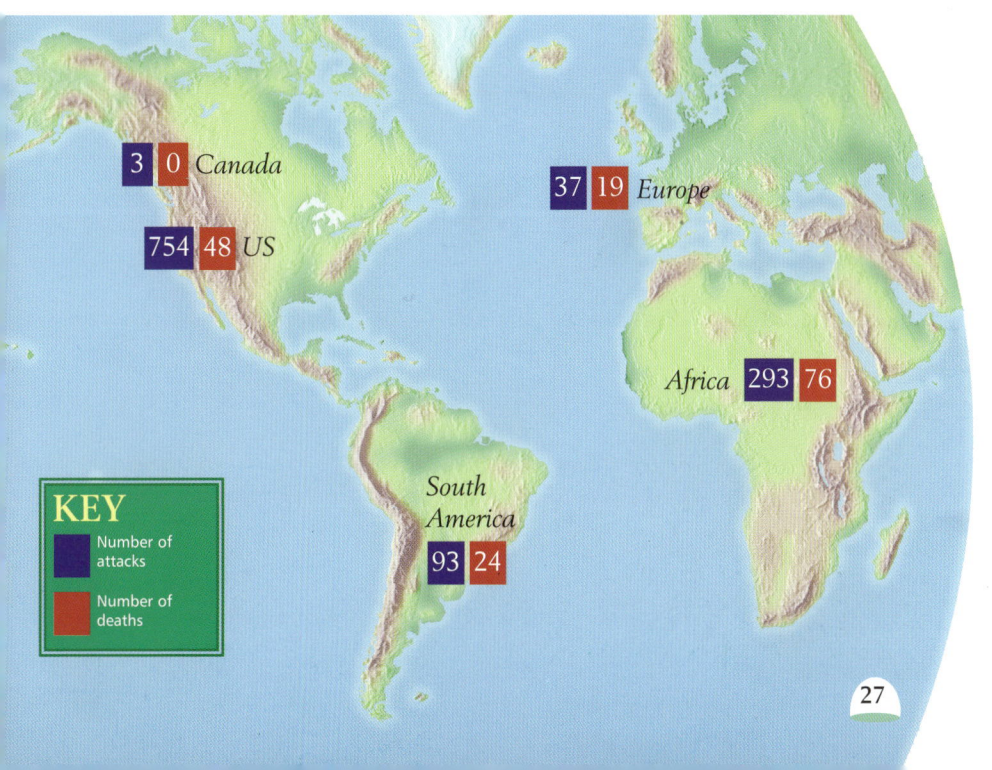

3 | 0 Canada

37 | 19 Europe

754 | 48 US

Africa 293 | 76

South America 93 | 24

KEY
- Number of attacks
- Number of deaths

Crocodiles have been around for about 240 million years. But of the 21 species of crocodiles alive today, only two are regular people killers: the Nile crocodile and the saltwater crocodile.

Saltwater crocodile

Stick, Rock, Crocodile?

Crocodiles live in knee-deep water and are hard to see amongst the rocks and weeds. They remain motionless and patient for hours until suddenly they launch themselves at their prey. Hurtling up to 10 metres up the riverbank, or 2 metres straight up into the air, they grab their prey and drag it back to the water to be drowned, shaken to bits and eaten.

Screams across the Swamp

In 1945, the saltwater crocodile was responsible for one of the most nightmarish encounters recorded between humans and animals. As World War II drew to a close, a thousand Japanese soldiers attempted a night-time retreat across a thick, dark swamp between Burma and Romree Island. Nearby, Allied troops listened in horror to the futile gunshots and terrible screams as the crocodiles had a feast. By daybreak only 20 of the Japanese soldiers were still alive.

Crocodile teeth can only grip, not chew. Crocodiles swallow prey whole or shake it into bite-sized pieces.

What a nightmare!

FACT FILE
From Nightmares ... to Phobias

KEY
- ◆ Phobia
- 💬 How You Say It
- 👀 Afraid Of . . .

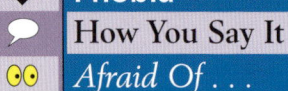

◆ **zoophobia**
- ZO-A-FO-BEE-A
- 👀 animals

◆ **arachnophobia**
- A-RACK-NA-FO-BEE-A
- 👀 spiders

◆ **ophidiophobia**
- O-FID-EE-A-FO-BEE-A
- 👀 snakes

◆ **cynophobia**
- SIGH-NA-FO-BEE-A
- 👀 dogs

◆ **ailurophobia**
- EYE-LOO-RA-FO-BEE-A
- 👀 cats

◆ **ornithophobia**
- OR-NI-THA-FO-BEE-A
- 👀 birds

◆ **alektorophobia**
- A-LECK-TA-RA-FO-BEE-A
- 👀 chickens

◆ **entomophobia**
- EN-TA-MO-FO-BEE-A
- 👀 insects

◆ **saurophobia**
- SAW-RA-FO-BEE-A
- 👀 lizards

Glossary

camouflage	the use of skin colours and markings to make an animal blend into its environment
fangs	long, sharp teeth through which venom is injected
inflating	puffing up, expanding or swelling
insomnia	inability to sleep
nervous system	system of nerves throughout an animal's body
paralyse	make unable to move
parasites	animals or plants that live on or in another animal or plant
repel	drive away or force back
spasm	a sudden muscle contraction
species	a group of animals or plants with similar characteristics or qualities
suffocates	dies because it can't get enough air
venom	poisonous fluid that animals such as spiders and snakes inject into their prey

inflating

INDEX

Page numbers in **bold** refer to photos or illustrations.

antivenom 11, 15
bloodsuckers 6, 7
box jellyfish 15, **15**
camouflage 24
crocodiles 28-29, **28**, **29**
   saltwater crocodile **28**
eels 22-23, **22**, **23**
   danger to divers from 23
   moray eel 22, **22**
fangs 10, **14**, 15
leeches 5, 6, **6**
   teeth, 6, **6**
lice 7, **7**
phobias 30
piranhas 21
sharks 26–27, **27**
   bull shark **26**
   great white shark **26**
   oceanic white tip shark **26**
   tiger shark **26**

snakes 12–19
   anaconda 18-19, **19**
   boa constrictor **18**, **19**
   carpet python **19**
   fangs **14**, 15
   Gaboon viper **15**
   jaws 17, **17**
   rattlesnake 13, **14**
   taipan 14, **14**, **15**
   tiger snake 15, **15**
   venom 15, 16, 18
spider webs 8, **9**
spiders 8–12
   black widow spider **10**
   Brazilian wandering spider 10, **10**
   golden orb-web spider 8, **9**
   Goliath bird-eating spider 8
   recluse spider **10**
   Sydney funnel-web spider 10, **10**, **11**
   wandering spider **11**
   wolf spider **10**
stonefish 24-25, **24**, **25**
venom 10, **14**, 15, 16, 18, 24, 25